The Sweet Problem of Baby Bears

AF593712

Dear Parents!

We warmly thank you for choosing our book on healthy nutrition. We firmly believe that books are a wonderful way to sensitize children to these important topics and to convey the effects of unhealthy eating habits in a playful manner.

Why is Sugar Not Good for Children?

Sugar has become a staple in our children‘s diets in recent years. It‘s present in almost all the products we buy. Excessive consumption has negative impacts on the health and well-being of our little ones.
Here are just a few reasons:

Development of Cavities: Excessive sugar consumption significantly increases the risk of cavities and dental problems in children.

Obesity: Sugar-laden foods and drinks are often calorie-rich but nutrient-poor. Excessive consumption can lead to weight gain and, in the long run, obesity.

Energy Dips and Concentration Issues: Sugar-filled snacks and sweets provide a temporary energy boost but also lead to rapid energy crashes and concentration problems in children (due to high glycemic index).

Addictive Potential: Sugar can create addiction and intensify cravings for sweet foods, leading to a vicious cycle.

Why is it Important to Educate and Inform Children?

Early education about a healthy lifestyle sets the foundation for a happy and healthy life for our children. The book about the healthy adventures of the bear cubs offers an entertaining and educational story, emphasizing the importance of balanced nutrition and moderate sugar consumption. The story sparks children‘s imagination and interest. Together, we can promote the health and well-being of our children and lay a solid foundation for a healthy and happy life.

ENJOY THE JOURNEY!

„Children are guests who ask for directions."

Maria Montessori

A dense green forest is on the banks of the river, home to a bear family.

Mama Bear,Papa Bear, and two cubs:

Teddy and Bella, lived in a land full of bears.

Papa Bear made sure his loved ones had everything they needed to live.

The cubs loved going on outings with him to catch fish.
Mama Bear and the cubs gathered fruits and herbs from the forest and grew crispy carrots in their garden. This way, the bear family always had a healthy meal on the table.

Mama Bear placed great importance on a healthy diet for her family. Their sustenance came from what nature provided.

They loved playing volleyball together.

Right in front of their house was a volleyball court,
where the Bear family regularly played to to have fun!

One day, Aunt Bearbel visited from across the river, from the Licorice Forest. Aunt Bearbel brought an entire bag of sweets!

This was something completely new for the cubs!

„Please, my darlings, enjoy something delicious!“ she encouraged the children. „Mmmm... delicious!“ the cubs exclaimed in unison.

They liked the fruity squeezies the most. Aunt Bearbel brought them a ton of sweets, and since then, the little bears and their parents snacked a little on the sweet treats every day.

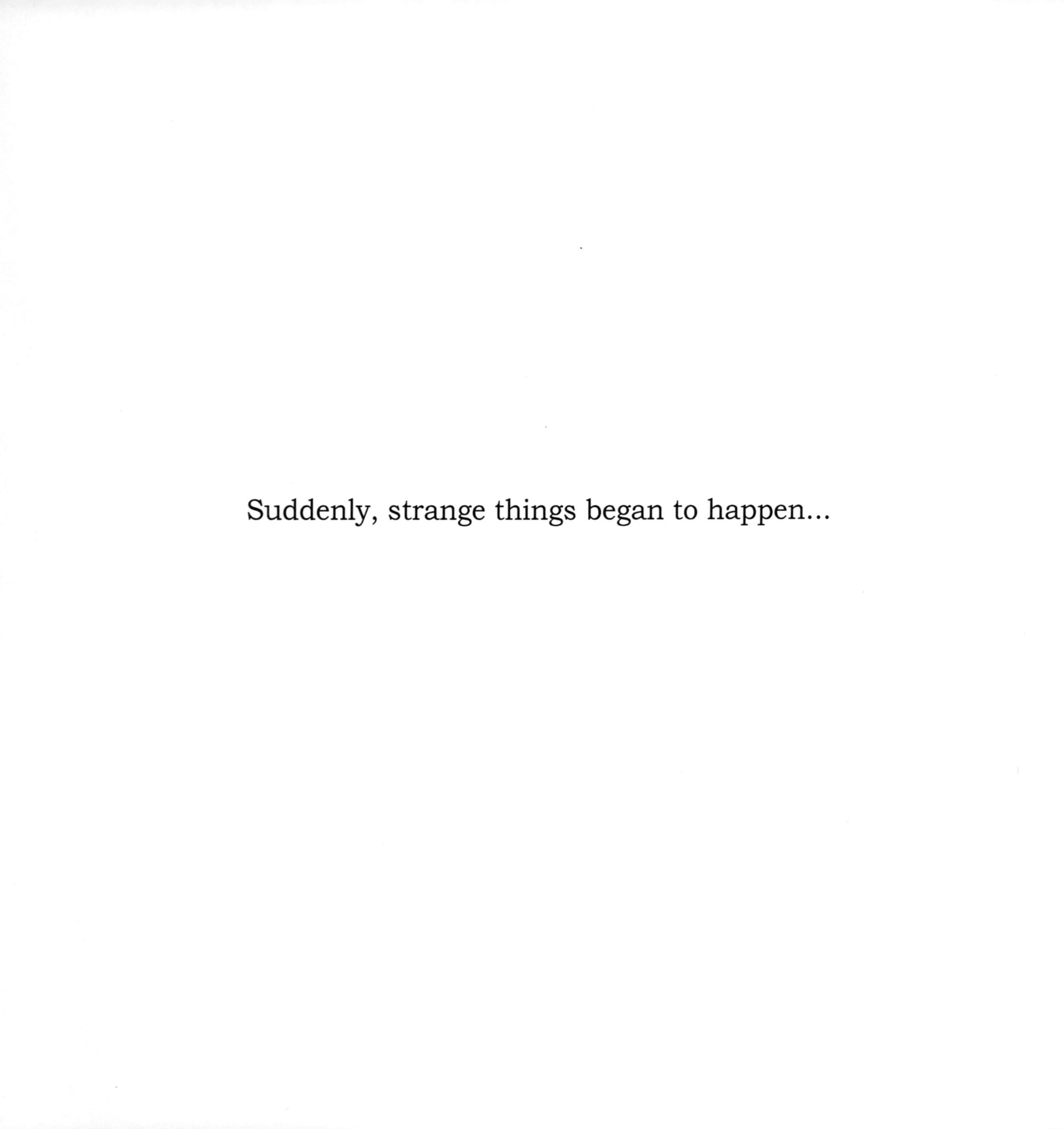

Suddenly, strange things began to happen...

The cubs lost their zest for life, they had no energy to run around, and their thoughts constantly revolved around Aunt Bearbel's bag of candy... Moreover, they always felt hungry and tired.

The cubs no longer had a taste for regular food.
The forest berries no longer appealed to them,
and the garden carrots remained untouched on their plates...

Mama Bear grew very concerned for her little ones and became quickly nervous and impatient. She scolded the cubs and easily flew into a rage...

The cubs sensed their mother behaving differently, and that made them very worried... They had never seen their mama like this before

They decided to find clues and uncover the reason behind these strange occurrences! „Oh, we must do something, our mama is acting oddly... as if she‘s not herself,“ Bella cub said.

„Calm down, I know someone who can help us!“
Bear cub comforted his brother.

In search of answers to these difficult questions, the little Bears set off to the wise Owl, who lived an hour away from their hut. For such a long journey, they took some provisions from Aunt Bear. Just in case they got hungry along the way. the long way.

The Bear cubs finally reached Owl.
Owl welcomed them and immediately showed them the contents of her baskets filled with sweets. She asked them if they would eat those too.
The teddy bear cubs eagerly replied,
„Yes, these fruity squeezies are great!“

The wise Owl sighed and explained to the bears what had happened. „These delicious fruity squeezies contain a lot of sugar, and this sugar is tricky. It‘s sweet and loved by all, but it robs one of energy and health. When consumed regularly, it‘s hard to give up because it tastes so good.“

„Are you saying that all this happened just because of this candy?“
the bears asked.
„Yes, I am most certain.“ the Owl concluded.

The wise Owl gave them valuable advice to help them return to their old lives. She told them to cut down on eating sweets and get back to healthy eating, emphasizing that candies should now be consumed in smaller amounts, and everything will return to how it was.

The first week with fewer sweets was tough for the bears,
but with their parents‘ help, they fought to return to their old lives.

And together, they decided:

FEWER SWEET SNACKS!

About Autors

Kangu Children's Books is founded by the parents of two wonderful children, with a background in education and a fascination for Montessori. Their goal is to create books that not only provide great entertainment but also help children (and parents) find answers to difficult questions, boost self-esteem, and convey important life information, making them the perfect material for both learning and play

We are grateful for your decision to purchase this book and sincerely hope that it meets your expectations. We value your feedback and look forward to hearing your thoughts, as they will assist us in our ongoing efforts to provide our customers with the highest level of satisfaction possible.

MORE FROM

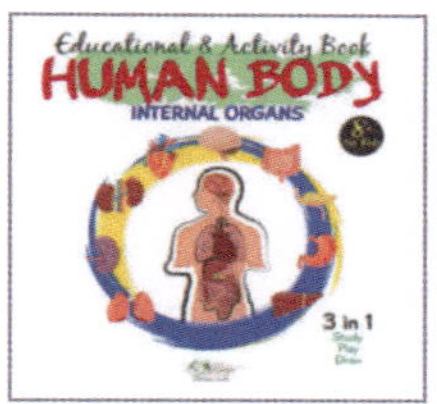

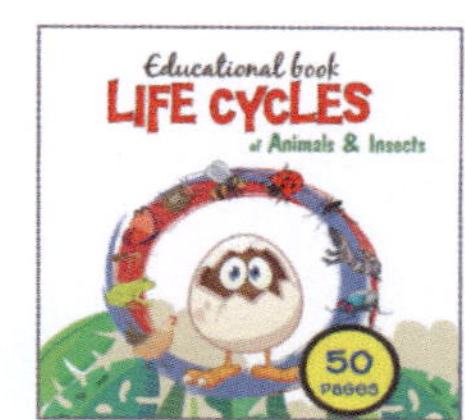

COPYRIGHT 2023 MATEUSZ GACEK

Publisher: Mateusz Gacek, Krummnussbaum, Austria
Contact: Kangu.trageberatung@gmail.com
www.kinga-gacek.at, wwww.bliskosciowytata.pl
Authors: Kinga & Mateusz Gacek
Illustrations: Michael Bachrach; michi.bachrach@gmail.com
Vertrieb: Amazon KDP Publishing

All rights reserved by the publisher
Any use is prohibited without the consent of the publisher

Printed in Great Britain
by Amazon